FEB 0 8

KN

ALY and AJ

Kathleen Tracy

P.O. Box 196
Hockessin, Delaware 19707
Visit us on the web: www.mitchelllane.com
Comments? email us: mitchelllane@mitchelllane.com

Mitchell Lane PUBLISHERS

Printing   1   2   3   4   5   6   7   8   9

A Robbie Reader
Contemporary Biography/ Science Biography

Albert Einstein	Albert Pujols	Alex Rodriguez
Aly & AJ	Amanda Bynes	Brittany Murphy
Charles Schulz	Dakota Fanning	Dale Earnhardt Jr.
Donovan McNabb	Drake Bell & Josh Peck	Dr. Seuss
Dylan & Cole Sprouse	Henry Ford	Hilary Duff
Jamie Lynn Spears	Jessie McCartney	Johnny Gruelle
LeBron James	Mandy Moore	Mia Hamm
Miley Cyrus	Philo T. Farnsworth	Raven-Symone
Robert Goddard	Shaquille O'Neal	The Story of Harley-Davidson
Syd Hoff	Tiki Barber	Thomas Edison
Tony Hawk		

Library of Congress Cataloging-in-Publication Data
Tracy, Kathleen.
  Aly and AJ / by Kathleen Tracy.
    p. cm. — (A Robbie reader)
  Includes bibliographical references (p.), discography (p.), filmography (p.), and index.
  ISBN-13: 978-1-58415-595-9 (library bound)
  1. Aly & A.J.—Juvenile literature. 2. Michalka, Alyson, 1989– —Juvenile literature. 3. Michalka, Amanda, 1991– —Juvenile literature. 4. Singers—United States—Biography—Juvenile literature. 5. Actresses—United States—Biography—Juvenile literature. I. Title.
  ML3930.A46T73 2008
  782.42164092'2—dc22
                                           2007023476

ABOUT THE AUTHOR: Kathleen Tracy has been a journalist for over twenty years. Her writing has been featured in magazines including *The Toronto Star's Star Week*, *A&E Biography* magazine, *KidScreen* and *Variety*. She is also the author of numerous biographies and other nonfiction books, including *Mariano Guadalupe Vallejo*, *William Hewlett: Pioneer of the Computer Age*, *The Watergate Scandal*, *The Life and Times of Cicero*, *Mariah Carey*, *Kelly Clarkson*, and *The Plymouth Colony: The Pilgrims Settle in New England* for Mitchell Lane Publishers. She divides her time between homes in Studio City and Palm Springs, California.

PHOTO CREDITS: Cover, pp. 10, 14—David Longendyke/ Globe Photos; pp. 4, 17, 24—Frazer Harrison/ Getty Images; p. 6—Noel Vasquez/ Getty Images; p. 7—Barry Talesnick/ Globe Photos; pp. 8, 26—Graham Whitby Boot/ Globe Photos; p. 13—Robyn Beck/ Getty Images; p. 18—John M. Heller/ Getty Images; pp. 20, 21—Paul Hawthorne/ Getty Images; p. 22—Chad Buchanan/ Getty Images

TABLE OF CONTENTS

Calling themselves "the twins born two years apart," Aly (left) and AJ have been inseparable since they were little. They have also shared a love of music. Aly says, "I think it started when we were three and five; just singing in church together and in school plays."

In Their Blood

Some people are born to be entertainers. Just ask sisters Aly and AJ. "We've been performing since before we can remember," Aly says. "We never thought it would become a career."

Their talents would also make them stars.

Alyson Renae Michalka (mish-AL-kah) was born on March 25, 1989. Amanda Joy was born April 10, 1991. Their first family home was in Torrance, California, which is near Los Angeles. They moved to Seattle, Washington, when AJ was still a baby.

"We were there about seven years because of our dad's business," AJ explains.

Aly and AJ's parents, Mark and Carrie, have been very supportive of the girls in helping their dreams come true. For several years the family lived in Seattle, Washington, because of Mark's job as a contractor. They moved back to Los Angeles so that Aly and AJ could pursue acting careers.

Aly and AJ's music has appeared in many Disney movies. "No One" was featured in *Ice Princess*. "Walking on Sunshine," originally recorded by Katrina and the Waves, is on the *Herbie: Fully Loaded* sound track.

Their dad, Mark, is a **contractor** (KON trak tur), which is someone who builds houses or buildings. Their mom, Carrie, helps Mark run his business. She used to sing in a Christian group called the J.C. Band. Carrie always encouraged her daughters' love of music.

Growing up, AJ and Aly were inseparable. Their favorite thing to do was sing. Their first concert was for their guinea pig, Brownie! When they were three and five, they started singing at church.

7

Aly (left) and AJ enjoy being role models and are proud of their Christian faith. "We don't ever want to preach or shove anything down people's throats," Aly says. "But AJ and I want our music to be inspiring." AJ adds, "We don't want to exclude anybody."

For a while, Aly attended Bellevue Christian Mack Elementary School. Later, after their careers began to take off, she and AJ were **homeschooled** by a **tutor**.

"We love the one-on-one with a teacher," Aly said, whose favorite subjects are history and language arts. They also enjoy home-schooling because they can help pick out the subjects they study.

Inspired by their mom, the girls learned to play the piano and the guitar. "AJ and I wanted to be like her when we were younger, so it really came from that."

When they got older, they started writing songs. "We never force the songwriting," Aly says. "It's always inspired by something that happened to us or one of our friends. It just kind of happens . . . which is nice because it comes from a totally pure place."

At first, though, writing music was really just for fun. It would soon become life-changing.

After their careers took off, both sisters were homeschooled. They enjoyed working with a tutor because they were able to help pick what they studied. Despite their success, Aly and AJ still live at home with their parents.

A New Passion

One day Carrie got a pamphlet in the mail advertising an acting class. As a joke, she put it on her husband's desk. To Aly, it was no laughing matter.

"I said, 'Mom, I beg you,'" Aly recalls. "I want to do this!"

Carrie and Mark were hesitant. "They wanted us to be normal kids," says Aly. "But AJ and I banded together and we got into it. We had tons of fun."

Several agents came to the class. They were impressed with the girls. "They were saying, 'Come move out to L.A.,'" Aly recalls.

Luckily, Mark needed to be back in the Los Angeles, or L.A., area for his business, so the family returned to California. They settled in Thousand Oaks.

"We packed up, moved, and it all fell together," says Aly. "It just happened naturally." She was in a number of children's theater productions at her church. As a result, the talented teen was a featured soloist on two recordings for WORD Music: "Jailhouse Rock" and "Meet Me at the Manger."

The girls still loved music, but at this point, they concentrated on acting. AJ's acting career took off before Aly's. Her first job was in a TV commercial for a department store. She also did some print modeling. Her picture appeared on the packaging for Disney and American Girl toys. Her big break came in 2002. She guest starred on the daytime drama *Passions*. Over the next three years, she appeared in several more TV series.

Things were more difficult for Aly. "I had been **auditioning** and auditioning," she admits.

AJ (right) says she never takes her success for granted, nor has stardom ever been her goal. "I try not to compare myself to other people. I take what has been given to me in regard to talents, and I work really hard at perfecting those talents. I seize the moment of each day and don't worry about whether or not I am going to get a part."

"But I could never book the jobs because of my braces."

Even so, Aly was happy for AJ. She never got discouraged, and she kept studying hard. Aly had faith she would eventually get her chance.

Aly (left) and AJ went on their first concert tour in 2005. They opened for The Cheetah Girls. They were promoting their debut album, *Into the Rush.*

The Mouse House

Finally, Aly did get a break. She auditioned for a new Disney Channel series called *Phil of the Future.* "I had just gotten my braces off, so I had this hope," she said.

The audition went well. "I was really proud of myself that I'd gotten that far," Aly recalls. But she was realistic. Unlike AJ, she had no professional acting experience. When her manager called to say she'd been hired, Aly couldn't believe it.

"I was crying and screaming. It was a huge thing for me to accomplish! I was really happy that Disney gave me a chance."

In the series, she plays Keely, Phil's best friend. The show first aired in the summer of 2004. It was an immediate hit. Phil is played by teen heartthrob Ricky Ullman. Ricky, who was born in Israel, also goes by his birth name, Raviv.

That was just the beginning. Disney wanted Aly and her sister to record an album. AJ was especially thrilled. "I grew up loving Disney," she says. "And suddenly I was a part of it. It was totally surreal."

They wrote, or cowrote, all the original songs on the album. "It's all things that have happened to us in real life," says Aly. "It's stuff that kids can relate to."

"I think people want to listen to positive music," AJ adds. "Listening to music that's uplifting is really important. Especially for people who are growing up."

Into the Rush was released in August 2005. Their single, "Do You Believe in Magic," was number one on Radio Disney. "No One"

AJ and Aly join *Phil of the Future*'s Ricky Ullman and Amy Bruckner at Disneyland's 50th Anniversary Celebration in Disney. Aly costarred in the Disney Channel series as Phil's best friend, Keely Teslow.

was featured in the movie *Ice Princess*. By the beginning of 2006, the album had sold nearly half a million copies, so the record company issued a special edition. The sisters would also be **nominated** for an American Music Award for Best Contemporary Inspirational (in-spuh-RAY-shuh-nul) Artist.

It was official. Aly and AJ were pop stars!

Despite their lifelong closeness, AJ (right) admits they occasionally take breaks from one another. "We definitely have our moments when we want our own space. But there's this awesome energy with us. There's never a dull a moment."

Two Awesome Worlds

Aly and AJ seemed to be working nonstop. When they weren't acting, they were singing. When they got off the concert stage, they went back in front of the camera.

In September 2005, the girls performed a concert in Hollywood. After that they starred in the movie *Cow Belles*. They played rich sisters forced to work for their father. In November 2005, they filmed *Haversham Hall* for the Disney Channel. In the show the sisters played . . . sisters! Again.

Then Aly and AJ spent December on tour with the Cheetah Girls. They loved performing live and meeting the fans, but Aly admits bouncing back and forth can be hard. "We just take it one day at a time," she says. "When we're on the road, we focus on our music and performing." At home, they focus on acting.

"We love doing both," adds AJ. "I really couldn't pick a favorite. You get two awesome worlds. You can't really compare them."

Despite their full schedules, they manage to live full lives. "We definitely make sure we

In March 2006, Aly appeared on MTV's *Total Request Live.* "We all have a special talent and passion," she says. "We just need the support of parents and friends to help us find it. And if you have a dream, always go for it and trust yourself."

AJ admits she once broke her toe dancing alone in her bedroom. The doctor fitted her with a padded cast that went up to knee. She says it was the most embarrassing injury she's ever had.

have time off to be with friends, relax, go to spas and **rejuvenate**," says AJ.

"All of this stuff is, to me, being a normal kid," Aly comments. "I always find time to relax. Go into my bedroom and read a book. Or talk to a friend on the phone. It's fun because I've always enjoyed doing a lot of activities. I get bored really easily."

As they have gotten older, Aly (left) and AJ have become more involved with charity work. In 2007, they attended the 18th Annual A Time for Heroes Celebrity Carnival. It would benefit the Elizabeth Glaser Pediatric AIDS Foundation.

Staying Grounded

Aly and AJ are openly **devout**, but they don't want to be labeled Christian singers. They love Disney, but they don't want to be typecast as teen idols. They want to make good music for *everyone.* In early 2007, they were working on their next album, *Insomniatic.* "It's going to have more of a rock feel," promised AJ. "It's still going to be Aly and I. It's just going to be a more grown-up Aly and I."

That maturity is also reflected in their volunteer work. The sisters serve as cochairs of the Child Advisory Board for Amber Watch, an organization dedicated to educate children on how to stay safe.

"I Am One of You," a song on *Into the Rush*, was inspired by the kidnapping of a young Florida girl from a car wash.

Aly and AJ model clothes in a charity event to find a cure for multiple sclerosis (skler-OH-sis). AJ says there is no sibling rivalry between her and Aly. "I think a best friend should really be like a support system, no matter what. My sister is there for me, supporting me in whatever I want to do."

"We just want to remind kids—and adults—without scaring them," Aly told *Christianity Today.* "We're trying to prevent this sort of thing from happening by teaching kids to make wise choices, to be aware of their surroundings.

"We're child safety advocates, we donate money to those causes and want people to know even the smallest amount of support can make a huge difference."

Unlike some other young stars, the sisters have remained humble. "We're all about staying grounded," Aly says. "It's **morphed** into this huge career thing. AJ and I have been blessed to be a part of it. Yet it's not our whole life."

And they want the best for each other.

"We get asked a lot about whether we're competitive," says AJ. "But we don't feel that way. We're totally there for the other person. When one does something, the other one's rooting them on."

Aly (left) thinks her sister has the more outgoing personality. "Amanda's the life of the party! She really takes charge in any situation. She's not, like, crazy or anything, but I think her personality is more bubbly."

They also promise they won't turn into diet-crazy party girls. "It's tiresome to go out to parties, fake your way through them and pretend you're having a good time," Aly says. Being true to their values is more important to them than being famous. "Praying about it and just asking God for help is really important," says AJ. "We have to live how we think is right and just go for it. Aly and I aren't going to change ourselves for anybody."

1989 Alyson Renae Michalka is born March 25.

1991 Amanda Joy "AJ" Michalka is born April 10.

1995 They begin taking piano lessons.

2000 AJ is cast in her first commercial.

2001 Aly is featured the WORD Music recording "Jailhouse Rock."

2002 AJ joins CBS series *The Guardian*. Aly records another solo for WORD Music, "Meet Me at the Manger."

2004 Aly stars in *Phil of the Future*. Aly and AJ sign with Hollywood Records.

2005 *Into the Rush* is released in August; they perform in Macy's Thanksgiving Day Parade November 24; Aly is nominated for a Young Artist Award for Best Performance in a TV Series (Comedy or Drama)— Leading Young Actress, for her part in *Phil of the Future*. They go on tour with the Cheetah Girls.

2006 The girls are nominated for American Music Award for Best Contemporary Inspirational Artist on September 19; *Acoustic Hearts of Winter* is released September 26; they are named to cochair the Amber Watch Foundation Children's Advisory Board and hold a concert December 10 to benefit the foundation.

2007 Their direct-to-DVD movie *Super Sweet 16: The Movie* is released in May; in July, their album *Insomniatic* is released; the girls join the NextFest concert tour with Corbin Bleu and Drake Bell from July to September.

Filmography

AJ

2007	*Super Sweet 16: The Movie*
2006	*Haversham Hall* (TV movie)
	Cow Belles (TV movie)
2005	*Kitty's Dish* (voice for animated series)
2004	*General Hospital* (series)
	Six Feet Under (series)
2003	*Oliver Beene* (series)
2002	*Passions* (series)
	Birds of Prey (series)
	The Guardian (series)

Aly

2007	*Super Sweet 16: The Movie*
2006	*Haversham Hall* (TV movie)
	Cow Belles (TV movie)
2005	*Now You See It . . .* (TV movie)
2004–2006	*Phil of the Future* (series)

Discography

2007	*Insomniatic*
2006	*Acoustic Hearts of Winter*
2005	*Into the Rush*
	"Do You Believe in Magic" (single)

Compilations

2005	*Herbie: Fully Loaded* (sound track)
	Girlz Rock
	Ice Princess (sound track)
	Jingle Jams
	Disney Mania, Vol. 3

auditioning (aw-DIH-shuh-ning)—trying out for parts.

contractor (KON-trak-ter)—someone who arranges all the types of workers needed to build a house or other building, such as carpenters, electricians, and plumbers.

devout (deh-VOWT)—deeply religious.

homeschooled (HOHM-skoold)—To be educated at home by a parent or tutor.

inspired (in-SPY-erd)—given encouragement or an idea.

morphed (MORFD)—changed.

nominated (NAH-mih-nay-tud)—chosen as a likely winner of an award.

rejuvenate (ree-JOO-veh-nayt)—to become refreshed.

tutor (TOO-ter)—a private instructor or teacher.

Books

While there are no other books for young readers about Aly and AJ, you might enjoy these other Contemporary Biographies from Mitchell Lane Publishers:

Kjelle, Marylou Morano. *Brittany Murphy.* Hockessin, Delaware: Mitchell Lane Publishers, 2007.

Leavitt, Amie Jane. *Dylan and Cole Sprouse.* Hockessin, Delaware: Mitchell Lane Publishers, 2008.

Leavitt, Amie Jane. *Raven-Symone.* Hockessin, Delaware: Mitchell Lane Publishers, 2008.

Mattern, Joanne. *Drake Bell and Josh Peck.* Hockessin, Delaware: Mitchell Lane Publishers, 2008.

Works Consulted

Aly & AJ in Concert. The Disney Channel, 2005.

AmberWatch Foundation. "Teen Superstars Aly and AJ Present 'Doin' Our Part for Kids,' a Concert Benefiting the AmberWatch Foundation." December 10, 2006. http://www.amberwatchfoundation.org/media_resources/release_display.asp?id=23

Argyrakis, Andy. "Away from the Rush." *Christian Music Today,* November 14, 2005. http://www.christianitytoday.com/music/interviews/2005/alyandaj-1105.html

Boyer, Ashley. "A Voice for This Generation." *Brio,* December 2006. http://www.briomag.com/briomagazine/entertainment/a0007094.html

Christian Activities—Youth Ministries. "Sister Duo Aly & AJ." October 20, 2005. http://www.christianactivities.com/youth/story.asp?id=5024

Christian Post–Lyrics. "Aly & AJ."
http://lyrics.christianpost.com/artist/
aly-and-aj.htm
Interlinc: Maximizing Music and Media in Youth Ministry, "Aly
& AJ," n.d. http://www.interlinc-online.com/artists/
index.html?p=2&id=
183&PHPSESSID=cd380d6731eebd6519e56c1925cad101
MSN, "Scholastic Interview, Nov 2004,"
http://groups.msn.com/PhiloftheFuture/
amscholastic.msnw
Pop Generation, "Aly & AJ"
http://www.popgeneration.com/zone/popgen/
team.php?team_id=107
The Star Scoop. "Aly and AJ Michalka."
n.d. http://www.thestarscoop.com/2006oct/
aly_and_aj.php
"Tweenage Riot." *Blender* magazine, June 2006. http://
www.blender.com/guide/articles.aspx?id=1937

On the Internet
Aly & AJ Music http://www.alyandaj.com/
Amber Watch Foundation
http://www.amberwatchfoundation.org
Hollywood Records, "Aly & AJ"
http://hollywoodrecords.go.com/alyandaj/index.html
My Space http://www.myspace.com/alyandaj
Radio Disney, "Aly and AJ"
http://radio.disney.go.com/artists/backstage/
alyandaj/bio.html